LIFE IN
ANCIENT
BRITAIN

FROM PREHISTORIC
TO ROMAN TIMES

Brian Williams

IMPORTANT DATES

PALAEOLITHIC (OLD STONE AGE)
c. 700,000–12,000 YEARS AGO

700,000 years ago	Evidence for tool-making humans in East Anglia
500,000 years ago	Hunters camp at Boxgrove, West Sussex
150,000 years ago	Last Ice Age across Europe begins
130,000 years ago	Neanderthal people cope with Ice Age
40,000 years ago	Modern humans live alongside Neanderthals
30,000 years ago	Neanderthals die out in Europe
26,000 years ago	Paviland cave burial, South Wales
12,800 years ago	Creswell Crags cave art, Derbyshire

▼ Before the last Ice Age. An artist's impression of a riverside scene at Swanscombe, Kent, around 250,000 years ago when Britain's climate was warm.

MESOLITHIC (MIDDLE STONE AGE)
c. 10,000–4500 BC

c. 10,000 BC	Ice Age ends in Britain and forests spread
c. 8700 BC	Star Carr hunters' camp, Yorkshire
c. 8500–7500 BC	Evidence of first people in Scotland
c. 7000 BC	Britain's oldest skeleton, from Gough's Cave, Somerset
c. 6500 BC	Britain becomes an island

NEOLITHIC (NEW STONE AGE)
c. 4500–2300 BC

c. 4000 BC	First farmers in Britain
c. 3500 BC	Causewayed enclosures (such as Windmill Hill, Wiltshire) and long barrows (such as West Kennet, Wiltshire)
3200–2700 BC	Skara Brae stone village, Orkney
c. 2800–2600 BC	Stone circles and monuments such as Stonehenge and Avebury
2700 BC	'Beaker' pottery

BRONZE AGE
c. 2300–700 BC

c. 2300 BC	Metal-working (copper and bronze) alongside stone technology
c. 2000 BC	Beaker burials
c. 1500 BC	Copper mining at Great Orme, North Wales
c. 1300 BC	Flag Fen wooden wheel

IRON AGE
c. 700 BC–AD 43

700 BC	Tribal 'kingdoms' and Celtic Iron-Age culture
600 BC	Brochs (stone forts) in Scotland
300 BC	Maiden Castle, Dorset, Britain's largest hill fort
55/54 BC	Julius Caesar leads the first Roman landings in Britain
AD 43	The Romans conquer southern Britain

HOW BRITAIN BEGAN

Some 9,000 years ago 'Britain' was still part of a wild, thinly populated European land mass. A marshy plain covered what is now the North Sea, and across it trekked bands of nomadic hunters. By approximately 6500 BC, rising sea levels finally flooded this plain, creating the British Isles. In this land of forests, rivers and bare hills traces of people were few and far between, yet humans had lived here for thousands of years.

The first people of Ancient Britain left little evidence of their passing, apart from a few bones, stone tools, outlines of campsites and glimpses of cave art. Later peoples marked the landscape, leaving Britain and Ireland with a heritage of remarkable Neolithic sites, such as Stonehenge. Ancient stones and mounds often conceal more secrets than they reveal, but we can deduce that Ancient Britons were people like us, with different but high-skill technologies, and beliefs and social structures that were in close harmony with the natural world.

To uncover the secrets of Ancient Britain we rely largely on scientists: archaeologists, botanists, geographers and geneticists. Science reveals our links to distant ancestors, and tells an intriguing detective story, helping us to picture life thousands of years ago from the evidence of bones, flakes of flint, deer antlers, broken pottery and rusted swords, and to people a lost landscape of brooding stones and windswept mounds.

DATING ANCIENT BRITAIN

In the 19th century, relative chronologies were established by 'stratification' – the study of artefacts, such as pottery, and their location in layers in the soil. Modern techniques include radiocarbon dating, accurate to about 50,000 years; it calculates the rate of decay of radioactive carbon 12 and carbon 14 in organic matter (such as wood or bone). Potassium-argon dating can help date rocks, while dendrochronology ('tree ring dating') can date wooden objects up to about 8,000 years old.

PREHISTORIC BRITAIN

When the Romans came to Britain 2,000 years ago, they could well dismiss the island peoples' ancient past as 'unknown', because it was unrecorded, and probably as 'barbarous' as the rites of the Druids whose temples Roman soldiers tore down.

Prehistoric Britain remained largely unexplored until interest was shown by 'antiquarians' such as the writer Sir Thomas Browne (1605–82), whose excavations in Norfolk revealed what he called 'sepulchrall urnes' (actually Anglo-Saxon burials). For most Christians at this time, 'prehistory' did not exist. Archbishop Ussher of Armagh (1581–1656) had calculated on biblical evidence that the world had been created by God in 4004 BC. And that was that.

By the 19th century, evolutionary theory and fossil discoveries suggested that the Earth was much older. The 'three age' system (Stone Age, Bronze Age, Iron Age), proposed in 1836 by Christian Thomsen of Denmark, is still used to describe European prehistory, though with reservations. Stone-Age people used other materials, such as bone and antler, and while metal-using was a 'progression' in one sense, older technologies overlapped with it. Bronze (an alloy of copper and tin) was first used for weapons and tools in the Middle East, reaching Britain by around 2000 BC. Iron, first worked in Asia Minor and China, reached the Aegean by 1000 BC and Britain by around 700 BC.

Popular interest in prehistory was aroused in the 19th century by revelations about the origins of fossils. Prehistoric Britain, 130 million years ago, lay partly beneath a warm ocean teeming with fish, molluscs and crustaceans. On land lived dinosaurs and other reptiles. When these animals died, their skeletons were occasionally preserved as fossils in rocks for millions of years. Fossil-hunters and farmers who dug up these mysterious stone-bones believed them to be the remains of dragons, human giants or animals drowned in the Bible Flood.

In 1824, William Buckland, Oxford professor of geology, revealed otherwise: the bones of *Megalosaurus* (found at a quarry in Oxfordshire) were, he declared, those of an extinct 'giant reptile'. Further proof that such strange creatures

▼ *Megalosaurus* was the first dinosaur to be given a scientific name, by William Buckland in 1824. This Jurassic predator was 9m (29ft) long, with powerful jaws.

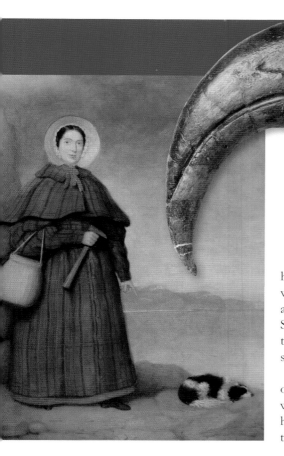

◄ This hook-claw (30cm/ 12 inches long) belonged to the fish-catching dinosaur *Baryonyx*. The claw was found in 1983 in a Surrey clay pit by amateur fossil enthusiast William Walker.

◄ Palaeontologist and fossil-hunter Mary Anning (1799–1847) made important geological finds in fossil beds in her home town of Lyme Regis, Dorset. Her cliff-searches provided new evidence of prehistoric life forms.

had once roamed Britain came from Mary Anning, who found *Icthyosaurus* in Dorset, and from Gideon and Mary Mantell, who discovered *Iguanodon* in Sussex. In 1841, geologist Sir Richard Owen coined the name 'dinosaur' (terrible lizard) for these sensational new animals.

Science had revealed that the world was much older than previously imagined. Dinosaurs had once wandered across Britain. As yet no one knew when humans first lived here, nor what kind of people they were.

FOSSIL SENSATIONS

Gideon Mantell (1790–1852) of Lewes in Sussex, a doctor and fossil-hunter, announced the discovery of *Iguanodon* in 1825, three years after publishing *Fossils of the South Downs,* a book illustrated by his wife, Mary. By the 1840s every museum in Britain was eager to display a skeleton, or even a bone or tooth, from a 'prehistoric monster'. Dinosaur statues in the 'prehistoric park' at Crystal Palace, unveiled in 1854, proved a popular sensation, even though they were anatomically inaccurate.

➤ This 1911 photograph shows the concrete dinosaur statues at Crystal Palace in south London. The dinosaurs were designed by William Waterhouse Hawkins (1807–94) with advice from leading expert of the day Sir Richard Owen.

Most scientists agree that our earliest ancestors came out of Africa, where 'pre-humans' lived more than 2 million years ago. Early humans (not yet modern *Homo sapiens*) had migrated into southern Europe by about 800,000 years ago, and Britain may have been home to some of northern Europe's earliest humans. By 700,000 years ago they were hunting and making flint tools in East Anglia, as revealed by recent finds at Pakefield (Suffolk) and Happisburgh (Norfolk).

By 450,000 years ago, groups of hunters at Boxgrove in West Sussex were making camps to butcher carcasses and make tools. Similar groups wandered across Britain, and out across the marshland of what is now the North Sea, following migrating herds of deer and horses, and returning every season to favourite campsites. A leg bone found at Boxgrove came from a well-built male around 1.8m (6ft) tall. His kit included wooden spears and flint hand-axes, all-purpose tools shaped to fit the hand, and used to cut skin, flesh and bone.

Another 250,000 years, and 'Swanscombe Man' was hunting along the Thames and nearby river valleys. The skull remains of this early human (actually a female), from the near-modern sub-species *Homo heidelbergensis*, were discovered in Swanscombe, Kent, in 1935–36. Amazingly, a matching fragment from the same skull turned up in 1955.

By around 40,000 years ago at least two species of humans lived in prehistoric Europe: *Homo sapiens* (more or less modern humans) and Neanderthals (named after a valley in Germany, where bones were found in 1856). Neanderthals were probably at least as intelligent as *Homo sapiens*: they used flint tools, made fire and buried their dead. Neanderthal remains have been found in Wales, and also in Norfolk where mammoth and woolly rhinoceros bones, hand-axes and worked flints unearthed at Thetford are believed to be Neanderthal. Although tough enough to survive the Ice Age, by 30,000 years ago the Neanderthals had died out, leaving the future clear for modern humans.

Prehistoric people had to be hardy to survive the perils of a nomadic hunting life, and to endure the glacial cold of the Ice Age, when mammoth, reindeer and woolly rhinoceros roamed an icy tundra landscape, and cave bears disputed ownership of gloomy caves with humans. In 2002, Whitemoor Haye in Staffordshire revealed the skeleton of a woolly rhino, between 30,000 and 50,000 years old. Woolly mammoth remains include the bones

THREE AGES OF MAN

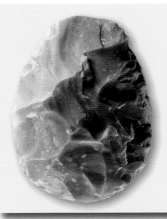

The Palaeolithic or Old Stone Age lasted over a million years, into the last Ice Age which had petered out by about 10,000 BC. Next came the Mesolithic or Middle Stone Age (a term normally referring to north-west Europe only), roughly 8000–3000 BC. The Neolithic or New Stone Age overlapped with the later Bronze and Iron Ages. The three ages feature changes in stone-tool technology, from chipped stones through to polished quality tools.

◀ A flint hand-axe, one of many tools found at Boxgrove. An all-purpose cutter, it could slice through hide and flesh.

THE PILTDOWN HOAX

In 1912, a skull 'found' at Piltdown (Sussex) caused a sensation. 'Piltdown Man' was hailed as the 'missing link' between apes and humans. In 1953, however, the skull was revealed to be a fake, a composite of orang-utan and medieval human bones. Suspicion for the hoax was directed at solicitor Charles Dawson (1864–1916), who 'found' the skull and after whom '*Eoanthropus dawsoni*' ('Dawson's dawn man') was at first named.

> ➤ Reconstructed head of 'Piltdown Man' (1950). Three years later, this 'missing link' in human evolution was exposed as a fake.

PILTDOWN

of an adult and three juveniles unearthed in a quarry at Condover near Shrewsbury (Shropshire) in 1986.

By about 13,000 years ago, the climate had warmed, causing the icecaps to retreat. With the change came a greener landscape and new fauna, such as elephant, rhinoceros, hippopotamus, deer and horse, a rich resource for human hunters.

> ◀ Artist's impression of a Neanderthal, the human species that for thousands of years co-existed with modern humans in Europe. Neanderthals were particularly well adapted to a cold climate.

> ➤ A woolly mammoth skull found in 2004 at Ashton Keynes in Wiltshire. Mammoths were adapted to Ice-Age cold, and may have survived in Siberia until about 4,000 years ago.

Prehistoric people thrived in Britain's post-glacial milder climate, though the population was probably only a few thousand. The oldest trees in Britain were cold-tolerant species such as pine and birch, but as the climate grew warmer, deciduous forest trees – including oak, elm, alder, lime and hazel – spread. Within this ancient wildwood, people hunted with spears and bows, snares and traps. Their quarry included red deer, elk, wild boar and horse, and the giant ox or aurochs. A massive beast with branching horns, the aurochs died out in Britain during the Bronze Age, though the white cattle in Northumberland's Chillingham Park (see page 13) may be descended from the aurochs or another wild ox.

Stone-Age hunters competed with animal predators, including bears, lynxes and wolves. Britain's largest-ever mammalian carnivore, the cave lion (bigger than a modern African lion), had died out around 13,000 years ago, as the Ice Age was coming towards its end. As people became herders and farmers, large predators were a threat to livestock and so were hunted to extinction. First to go was the bear, probably in pre-Roman times. The lynx was extinct by the Norman Conquest. The wolf survived the Middle Ages: the last British wolf was killed in Scotland in 1743.

Hunting was a communal activity, relying on teamwork to stalk, trap or ambush prey often much bigger and stronger than a single human. Hunters' camps, such as the one found by archaeologists at Star Carr, in Yorkshire's Vale of Pickering, show how Mesolithic people lived. Hunters first camped at Star Carr beside a lake around 11,000 years ago, returning from season to season to make tools and weapons – typically small flint blades

HORN DANCERS?

Intriguingly, the people at Star Carr may have dressed up like the Staffordshire Abbots Bromley Horn Dancers, who still perform their ancient folk dance today, wearing deer antlers. Remains of deer skulls at Star Carr look like antlered headdresses. Were these worn for shamanistic ritual? Or for camouflage while stalking deer?

◄ Part of a horn from an aurochs. This wild ox was bigger than modern farm cattle, with forward-curving horns. Its ferocity meant most hunters gave it a wide berth, yet the aurochs died out in Britain during the Bronze Age.

◄ Stone-Age hunters killed beaver for their pelts, along with other fur-bearing animals such as fox and marten. Beavers died out in Britain during the 16th century, but this animal is part of a reintroduction programme in Scotland.

► Mesolithic hunting weapons. Spears and barbed harpoons were fashioned from wood tipped with antler or bone. Hunting required teamwork, patience and courage to bring down a wild ox or an elk.

COASTAL CALAMITY

Some 8,000 years ago, the catastrophic Storegga Slides landslips in Scandinavia created a tsunami wave perhaps 25m (82ft) high, flooding across the North Sea. The wave drowned the last land-bridge across 'Doggerland', completing the filling of the North Sea. It inundated stretches of the British coast, where the impact on Mesolithic coastal communities can be imagined.

▲ A fragment of amber (23mm/0.9 inches long) found at Star Carr. Dating from around 8000 BC, it may have been worn as an ornament, perhaps as part of a necklace.

◄ Deer skull from the campsite at Star Carr. Antler headdresses might have been hunters' camouflage or worn in ritual dances in the hope of good hunting and full bellies.

called microliths. In 2008, archaeologists at the site found what is claimed to be Britain's oldest house, a wooden post-supported structure from about 9000 BC.

Stone-Age people exploited every available food source. Coast-dwellers fished with bone hooks, harpoons and nets, and climbed cliffs to take seabirds and collect eggs. Some groups living close to the shore ate shellfish, such as mussels, and discarded mollusc shells in vast heaps or 'middens'; a midden at Morton in Fife had at least 10 million shells. Nuts were a nutritious staple food, and a pit studied in the 1990s at Colonsay in the Hebrides contained thousands of roasted hazel-nut shells.

Caves were shelters and probably also sacred places. In 1823, William Buckland found human bones in Goat's Hole Cave at Paviland on the South Wales Gower Peninsula. The 'Red Lady' of Paviland was in fact a man, aged 25 to 30, who died about 26,000 years ago. Buried with him were a bracelet of mammoth-tusk ivory, a pendant made from a periwinkle shell, other shells, ivory rods and three spatulas made of bone. He had worn a two-piece garment, and his skin had been stained with red ochre. Intriguingly, his head had been removed.

Not long after the Paviland burial, Britain's last great Ice Age began. Intense cold made life precarious and sent people into caves, such as Gough's Cave in Cheddar Gorge, Somerset. First excavated in the 1890s, Gough's Cave

produced fresh surprises in 1986: human bones (at least three adults and two children), jumbled among flints, antlers, bits of ivory and animal bones. Cut marks on the human bones suggested the corpses had been dismembered after death.

Caves were places to commune with the personal and spirit worlds through art. By the light of lamps burning animal fat, or faint sunlight from the cave mouth, artists painted and scratched images of the animals that shared their world. In 2003, Britain's most startling prehistoric rock-art was revealed at Creswell Crags, a limestone gorge not far from Sheffield. Here are a number of caves which were occupied by Neolithic hunters from around 43,000 BC. The caves contained remarkable objects such as the rib bone of a horse,

The Paviland cave burial, pictured as it may have happened some 26,000 years ago. Caves were places to shelter, but some at least also became places of special significance.

engraved with a horse's head. On the walls were engravings, earlier dismissed as graffiti (and even added to by visitors). The pictures were in fact Britain's oldest cave art, comparable to the cave paintings at Lascaux in France and Altamira in Spain. Working 12,800 years ago, the artists made skilful use of uneven rock surfaces, creating realistic outlines of animals such as ibex and bison, plus part of a goat and what look like birds, though some people interpret the 'birds' as 'dancing women'.

Later in date than Creswell's cave pictures, but more numerous, are the 'cup and ring' rock engravings of Northumberland. More than a thousand of these abstract designs were cut into rocks between 6,000 and 3,500 years ago. Why they were made remains a mystery.

⋏ Enigmatic rock art from Creswell Crags. These angular figures might be birds, women or geometric shapes.

➤ Thigh bone from the 'Red Lady' of Paviland, the oldest known burial of a 'modern human' in Britain.

◄ A Stone-Age artist at work. This artist's impression shows how a flint tool was used to engrave animals into the rock of a cave wall.

ANCESTRAL CONNECTIONS

In the 1990s, DNA tests on the Gough's Cave human remains provided evidence of surprising direct links to the distant past. Samples dating from 11,000 to 7000 BC showed a genetic link to people in the present, matching DNA samples taken from a local teacher and two of his pupils. 'Cheddar Man' was alive and well, and living in Somerset.

BRITAIN'S FIRST FARMERS

From around 4000 BC, Britain's first farmers began to clear patches of forest with stone axes for livestock-grazing and crop-sowing. The move to farming was a gradual shift, in tune with a gentler climate, and brought enormous changes. Nomads became residents of villages with defences to safeguard permanent homes, fields and livestock. Hunting and gathering of wild foods continued but a more complex community was now served by specialists: potters, weavers and metal-workers.

The first crops grown in British soil were cereals, principally emmer wheat and barley. Later farmers grew flax, for linen. The forest was cleared by 'slashing and burning' small plots, which were planted and harvested for a few seasons, then abandoned. People still gathered edible roots and leaves, supplemented by wild fruits such as blackberries, sloes, crab apples and hazelnuts. They also cultivated food-plants such as peas and beans. At Scord of Brouster in Shetland, there are three circular stone houses and half a dozen small, walled fields, from which surface stones were removed into neat heaps and rows. Such allotment-type plots were probably typical of many early farmsteads.

By 3000 BC, ditches and banks marked out bigger fields for cattle. Domestic cattle (and probably sheep and goats too) were introduced from continental Europe. The cattle were longhorns, smaller and less aggressive than the fierce native aurochs. Most cattle were slaughtered for meat when two or three years old; they provided hides (for leather), sinews, horns and bones. Wild horses had long been hunted, but horses may have been herded semi-wild, perhaps by hand-rearing foals of mares killed for food. The Exmoor pony is thought to be the British native horse. Taming the horse for riding and

⌄ Two mainstays of the first farms were emmer wheat and beans, here being grown in a recreated Neolithic field at Butser Ancient Farm in Hampshire.

⌃ This sickle is the kind used by Neolithic farmers at harvest-time. The flint blade was found in the River Thames. The wooden handle is modern.

▲ The white cattle of Chillingham Park, Northumberland, possibly descendants of the wild aurochs. British Neolithic farmers domesticated smaller, more docile cattle breeds, imported from Europe.

▼ Soay sheep of the Western Isles are probably close in appearance to the sheep of Neolithic herds. Wild sheep were not native, so sheep were imported to Britain.

DOGS AND CATS

Dogs accompanied hunters and herders. From around 8000 BC, bone-finds suggest people had Labrador-sized dogs, probably still wolf-like, but also smaller terrier-types. Dogs were useful flock-herders, watchdogs and (as grain-storage developed) rat-catchers, and some dogs were no doubt family pets. Though the wild cat is native to Britain, there were no domestic cats on the first British farms. Domestic cats were introduced to Europe around 1000 BC, from the Mediterranean.

transport, however, did not happen until the Iron Age, over 2,500 years ago.

Sheep and goats were herded for wool and milk, as well as meat. Prehistoric sheep were wiry animals, probably resembling the Soay breed of St Kilda in the Hebrides. Goats, even hardier than sheep, became widespread too. The Neolithic pig was easy to keep in woodland, where it foraged like the wild boar, but it was not a long-distance seasonal traveller (unlike cattle, sheep and goats); pigs were, though, well suited to the more settled way of life developing, especially in southern Britain.

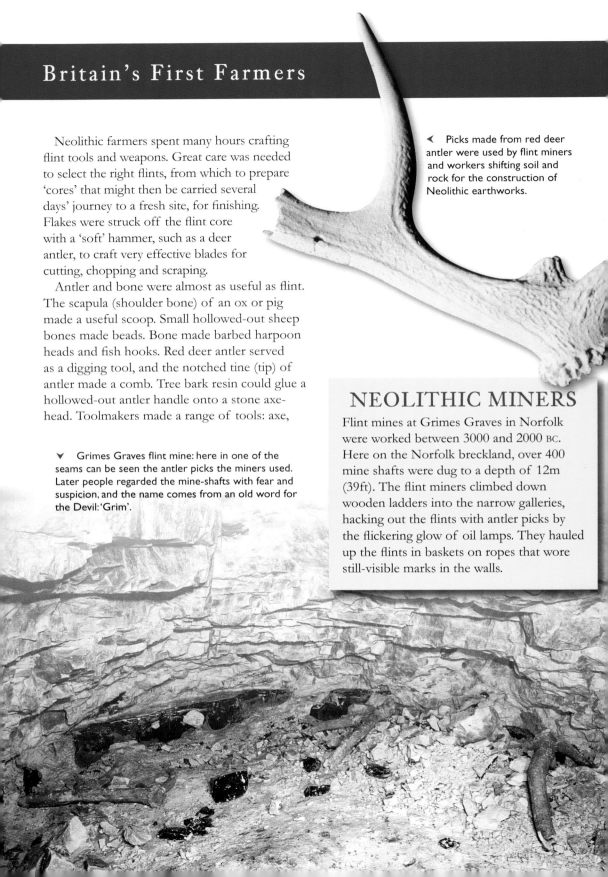

Britain's First Farmers

Neolithic farmers spent many hours crafting flint tools and weapons. Great care was needed to select the right flints, from which to prepare 'cores' that might then be carried several days' journey to a fresh site, for finishing. Flakes were struck off the flint core with a 'soft' hammer, such as a deer antler, to craft very effective blades for cutting, chopping and scraping.

Antler and bone were almost as useful as flint. The scapula (shoulder bone) of an ox or pig made a useful scoop. Small hollowed-out sheep bones made beads. Bone made barbed harpoon heads and fish hooks. Red deer antler served as a digging tool, and the notched tine (tip) of antler made a comb. Tree bark resin could glue a hollowed-out antler handle onto a stone axe-head. Toolmakers made a range of tools: axe,

◄ Picks made from red deer antler were used by flint miners and workers shifting soil and rock for the construction of Neolithic earthworks.

▼ Grimes Graves flint mine: here in one of the seams can be seen the antler picks the miners used. Later people regarded the mine-shafts with fear and suspicion, and the name comes from an old word for the Devil: 'Grim'.

NEOLITHIC MINERS

Flint mines at Grimes Graves in Norfolk were worked between 3000 and 2000 BC. Here on the Norfolk breckland, over 400 mine shafts were dug to a depth of 12m (39ft). The flint miners climbed down wooden ladders into the narrow galleries, hacking out the flints with antler picks by the flickering glow of oil lamps. They hauled up the flints in baskets on ropes that wore still-visible marks in the walls.

> This elegant polished axe-head is made of jadeite, a form of jade quarried in Italy. The effort needed to make and transport such rare objects meant they were highly valued as gifts and offerings.

adze, chisel, knife, scraper, awl and bone drill. Everyday tools were still being made of stone long into the metal age.

Baskets were made from pliable twigs and reeds, using the same weaving technique that produced mats and sheep hurdles. Strong string or rope could be created from twisted heather, wild clematis and honeysuckle, with plaited rawhide taking the strain of hauling heavy stones or logs. Every tree was known, and its uses; the oldest known English bows, from Somerset (about 3400 BC), were made from yew, just like the later medieval longbow. Wood made spears and harpoons, throwing sticks (for killing birds), ploughs and spades.

Most of the best flint came from the south of England (from Findon, near Worthing in West Sussex, for instance), but there were 'tool-factories' in Cumbria, the Highlands and Norfolk. The extent of tool-making sites such as Oakhanger in Hampshire, which yielded over 100,000 artefacts, mostly debris from tool-making, shows how generations of people worked there.

People walked long distances to trade flints, and water was no barrier to trade. Even around 8,000 years ago, seafarers in canoes or coracles were visiting the Scottish island of Rum, to collect 'bloodstone' (a form of silica) prized for making polished axes. Ireland and Britain were separated by rising sea levels some time after 7500 BC, so crossing the Irish Sea necessitated the building of log-craft or skin-boats.

Polished axes were traded across Britain from Great Langdale in Cumbria and the Preseli Hills in Wales. Axes seem to have had added value, as gifts and as offerings to gods. More than 350 stone axes have been found in the River Thames, presumably thrown there intentionally.

THE SWEET TRACK

Stone-Age people occasionally built footpaths, like the single-file Sweet Track footpath in Somerset (named after its 1970 finder, Raymond Sweet). The wooden pathway, which is 1.8km (just over a mile) long, was made around 3800 BC to allow people to cross boggy ground to a drier patch. A rare jadeite axe-head (possibly from Switzerland) was found in the bog. Surely too precious to be lost, was it dropped as an offering?

> A preserved section of the Sweet Track wooden pathway.

LIFE AND DEATH

Farming changed the landscape, and not just through field-creation, for settled communities made lasting structures, for both the living and the dead. The Neolithic period produced some of Britain's most atmospheric prehistoric monuments: stone cairns, hilltop 'causewayed camps', earthworks or 'henges', stone circles, mounds and burial chambers or barrows.

Farming could provide a more reliable food supply, but it was back-breaking work, and a failed crop or lost livestock could mean disaster. Fields were tilled by hand, or with a wooden plough dragged by an ox. Seed was hand-sown, and the ripe grain harvested with flint-tipped sickles. Threshing and winnowing was dusty work, followed by grinding on saucer-shaped stone querns to make gritty flour. Grain-flour was eaten

NEOLITHIC STYLE

Clothing is even more perishable than wood, and little evidence of Neolithic fashions survives: later Bronze-Age burials in Denmark suggest that women wore skirts, with a tunic or bodice, and kept their hair tidy with bone or antler pins. Men wore tunics and cloaks. Textiles (wool and linen) gradually replaced animal skins, though in winter furs and leather must have been essential to keep warm and dry. Footwear varied from leather moccasins to strips of cloth or deerskin wrapped around the foot.

as gruel or porridge, or baked into flat bread on hot stones beside a fire.

Fires were lit by friction, rubbing sticks or using a bowdrill to catch dry moss and leaves, but one fire in every village was probably kept burning whenever possible. Hunters and travellers may have carried fire with them, in a

◄ A pot from Windmill Hill (Wiltshire). The style is simple and the decoration minimalist.

➤ An artist's impression of Neolithic farmers bringing in the harvest.

A reconstruction of a Neolithic house, showing the frame, roof and walls of animal hides, and a central fireplace. Little trace of such all-organic homes survives, except – in a few cases – post-holes.

smouldering ball of dry moss wrapped inside a skin pouch.

Clay pots replaced the animal-skin bags previously used to carry and store liquids. British pottery was first made about 3800 BC; it was hand-shaped without using a wheel, and sun-dried before baking in a fire. Most early pots had round bases, flatter bases appearing later, perhaps to stand on a ledge or table. Pots were decorated by incising the wet clay with a bone tool or a twisted cord, or by impressing with a fingernail, though most Ancient British pots are plainer than ones made in continental Europe.

The homes of the first farmers had wood-pole frames, covered with animal hides or walled with wattle and daub (woven sticks plastered with mud and cow dung). Turf or thatch provided alternative roofing for larger structures, and the overhanging eaves gave shade in summer, and kept rain off the walls.

Where trees were scarce, Neolithic people built in stone. Knap of Howar on the Orkney island of Papa Westray is one of the oldest stone houses in northern Europe, inhabited from about 3500 BC. Equally remarkable is Skara Brae in Orkney, a stone village dating from between 3200 and 2700 BC. Skara Brae was uncovered in 1850 by a storm that laid bare a prehistoric settlement beneath sand dunes. The ten-house complex seems to have been communal, with a series of linked rooms within dry-stone walls, probably once roofed with driftwood, whale bones, turf and bracken. Inside the rooms were seats, beds, shelves and water-basins all made from stone.

Skara Brae: this building may have been a workshop where stone tools were made.

LIFE AT SKARA BRAE

At Skara Brae, people lived mainly on meat, milk and shellfish, especially limpets. They enjoyed some leisure time, playing with dice made from walrus-tusk ivory, and with knucklebones. They made pendants and beads from stone, bone, cow teeth and ivory, and may have gone in for cosmetics, perhaps face-painting.

➤ Bone and tooth jewellery was made by the island folk of Skara Brae some 5,000 years ago.

◄ The inner chamber of the West Kennet long barrow, restored to something like its original appearance. This large barrow contained the bones of 46 adults and children.

slabs from which a passage is angled to let the midwinter light shine into the central chamber.

Burial mounds or barrows dotted the landscape too, especially in the south. Barrow-building was at its height between 3800 and 2800 BC. These early long barrows, such as West Kennet and Winterbourne Stoke in Wiltshire, seem to have been family tombs, or perhaps for important people from related families. West Kennet long barrow is huge, 107m (350ft long), but most barrows are smaller. Long barrows often contained loose bones, with skulls resting in a separate part of the chamber. Perhaps bodies were first exposed for scavengers (such as crows and kites) to strip flesh from bones before being interred, usually at one end of the chamber, facing east. A total of 15 long barrows can be found within an hour's walk of Stonehenge – making the landscape richer in prehistoric remains than any other area of similar size in Britain.

Physically, Neolithic farmers looked like us. But to be over 40 was to be old, and the bulk of the population was between 15 and 30 years old. Death was as much a part of everyday experience as eating and drinking, and the ancestors were a constant spiritual presence in the landscape.

People following settled lives as farmers began burying their dead in a 'settled' place too, usually communally, under piles of stones called cairns or in timber burial chambers beneath earth-mound barrows. Britain has 600 or so megalithic (stone-built) tombs, more than half of them in Scotland, but many more must have vanished over time. The simplest are stone slab structures, like the dolmens at Zennor Quoit and Trethevy Quoit in Cornwall. Others are impressive and more complex chamber-tombs, such as the passage graves of Ireland, North Wales and Scotland. Maeshowe in Orkney, from around 2850 BC, is a fine example: a stone chamber tomb 25m (115ft) across, formed by three massive rock

HAUNTED BARROWS

Fanciful people in later times imagined barrows to be haunted by ghosts, or stacked with gold guarded by dragons. Barrow names such as Giant's Chair and Devil's Den (Wiltshire) reinforced their eerie presence in the landscape, though Hetty Pegler's Tump (Gloucestershire) is more homely, named after a 17th-century landowner. Ghost stories did not deter tomb-raiders like Dean Meriwether who in 1849 dug into 35 barrows in 28 days – the archaeological equivalent of big-game hunting!

A fragment of the Iceman's grass cape, which he wore over a deerhide tunic. His kit included a copper axe, a flint dagger, a bow and quiver of arrows, and a first-aid lump of 'medicinal' fungus. Neolithic Britons probably took much the same equipment when travelling.

DEATH IN THE MOUNTAINS

A frozen corpse found in 1991 in a melting glacier on the Italian-Austrian mountain borders gave new insight into how Neolithic people lived – and died. 'Otzi the Iceman' died about 5,300 years ago, the victim (evidence suggests) of human attack, not Alpine blizzard. His clothing included a bearskin cap, cape of plaited grass and shoes with bearskin soles and deerhide uppers, stuffed with grass. Such winter-wear would have been common across northern Europe.

Barrow-type graves for single burials continued through the Bronze Age. Round barrows were single tombs, presumably for important people; as well as round barrows, there were bowls, bells and ponds (which from the air look a bit like doughnuts). Mound-grave burials went on far beyond the Roman period: the Sutton Hoo ship burial in Suffolk, for example, dates from the AD 600s. Many barrows were excavated in the 19th century, and grave-objects removed – weapons, jewellery, bones, cremation urns. Barrows are often shown on maps as 'tumuli', from the Latin *tumulus* meaning 'mound'.

▼ Belas Knap long barrow in Gloucestershire. Dating from 3000 BC, and restored to something like its original appearance in the 1930s, it contained little when examined – perhaps having been 'investigated' in Roman times.

A Neolithic traveller trudging past the grass-covered barrow-mounds of Wessex would have been startled by the sheer scale of the enclosure on Wiltshire's Windmill Hill. It was a massive 'arena', 350m (1,150ft) across, with three rings of ditches crossed by causeways. Dating from about 3300 BC, though the site is older, Windmill Hill is the biggest 'causewayed camp' in the British Isles. Here and at similar sites such as Hambledon Hill in Dorset, people probably gathered, to renew friendships, to trade tools and animals, to marry and perform rituals. Such enclosures were meeting places for the living, not sepulchres, though the dead in their tombs were seldom far away.

The 'ritual landscape' of Ancient Britain had a religious, seasonal and ceremonial context that remains elusive – there are no written records to tell us what went on. But it is reasonable to assume that local communities ('clans' or tribes) lived in territories, and marked their landscapes with 'monuments' such as barrows and cairns,

▼ Windmill Hill today. The causewayed enclosure that stood here 5,000 years ago was probably a Neolithic meeting place.

▲ Neolithic stones in Cornwall: the Merry Maidens.

TURNED TO STONE

The 19 Merry Maidens are standing stones near Land's End in Cornwall. The stones are said to be the petrified remains of local girls lured away by two pipers while on their way to church one Sunday. For dancing on the Sabbath, the poor girls were turned to stone, and so were the pipers. A similar legend surrounds The Hurlers of St Clear. When players refused to stop their Sunday game of Cornish hurling at the demand of a local saint, they met the same fate as the Merry Maidens.

HIDDEN TREASURES

In 1833, a gold cape was found in a grave at Bryn yr Ellyllon (the Fairies' or Goblins' Hill) at Mold in North Wales. The Mold cape is one of the most remarkable long-hidden treasures of Ancient Britain, as is the Rillaton gold cup, found in 1837 on Bodmin Moor in Cornwall by workers pillaging a burial cairn for stone.

➤   The Rillaton cup, now in the British Museum in London, came from a Bronze-Age tomb. Its design suggests Mediterranean influence. A similar cup was found at Ringlemere in Kent in 2001.

standing stones (megaliths) and henges. A henge was a circle or oval (or, less often, a horseshoe), defined by a bank and ditch. At Stonehenge the bank is, untypically, inside the ditch. The recurring shape seems to reflect a belief that circles had special significance.

A monument's setting, and what could be seen from it, was seemingly as important as its scale, irrespective of the challenges of construction. A monumental architecture stretched from the far north of Britain in Orkney south to the downlands of Wessex, and has left us some of Europe's most remarkable Neolithic and Bronze-Age sites.

Wessex seems to have had special significance even before the first Stonehenge was built some 5,000 years ago. Here are some of the largest 'prehistoric monuments', such as the enigmatic mound of Silbury Hill, and The Cursus near Stonehenge, a processional way or boundary over 100m (109 yards) wide and

almost 3km (1.8 miles) long. In Wessex, too, are Stonehenge and the neighbouring stone circle at Avebury, which stand at the convergence of ancient ridgeways, travellers' tracks following dry ridges across country.

It took organized communal effort to create these landmarks, to haul stones over hill and dale, and across sea and river, and then to erect them at selected spots to form circles – circles of invitation to some people, but of exclusion perhaps to others. Succeeding generations added to or rebuilt the landmarks of their ancestors, so that many remained places of meaning and power for hundreds of years, and still retain their capacity to awe the onlooker.

➤   The Devil's Den near Marlborough in Wiltshire. These ancient stones are the remnants of a long barrow, now vanished.

STONEHENGE

About 100 henges survive in Britain. The biggest are in Wessex: Avebury, Durrington Walls, Mount Pleasant and Marden, which is some ten times bigger than Stonehenge in area, though now minus its stones. Even world-famous Stonehenge is but an echo of what it was in its prime.

Around 4,000 years ago, this ring of stones dominated the landscape. There were a lot of very large stones, most of them dressed to shape by pounding with stone hammers. The outer ring, the Sarsen Circle, originally had 30 stones crowned by 30 lintels; the uprights weigh about 25 tonnes, the lintels 7 tonnes. The 60 bluestones in the inner circle were brought from Wales, a distance of about 385km (240 miles), and 19 more form the Bluestone Horseshoe. The five Sarsen Trilithons were even more massive: two stones weighing 45 tonnes with a third stone across them. At the very heart was the Altar Stone, from Pembrokeshire, once upright but now buried beneath fallen stones.

Stonehenge was created in phases. About 3000/2800 BC there was a circular earthwork, ringed by wooden posts in holes (the 'Aubrey

Holes', after John Aubrey who recorded them in the 17th century). The entrance to the Avenue was marked by the 35-tonne Heel Stone, and the Slaughter Stone (now fallen). The entrance to Stonehenge was aligned with midsummer sunrise.

The second phase (2500/2100 BC) brought the first stone circles, beginning with the bluestones from the Preseli Hills in Wales. These stones (about 4 tonnes each) were set in two circles, with an entrance looking along the Avenue. The third phase, about 2000 BC, produced the Trilithon Horseshoe and the Sarsen Circle, and this was

WHAT WAS STONEHENGE?

Was Stonehenge a cemetery, temple, place of sacrifice, solar calendar or observatory? Possibly it was all of these at different times. Medieval historian Geoffrey of Monmouth thought the stones a memorial to Celtic-Britons slain by Saxons. In the 1960s, professors Gerald Hawkins and Fred Hoyle theorized it was a Neolithic 'computer' for predicting astronomical events. Most experts agree the sun was probably crucial to what went on here, with ceremonies at midsummer and midwinter. Feasts seem to have been a feature, with roast pork a favourite.

▼ Stonehenge today. It is not easy to picture the rings of stones as they were originally, though modern reconstructions have been made. The lintel stones are held in place with woodworking-style joints (mortice-and-tennon, tongue-and-groove).

Part of the Bluestone Horseshoe, transported on rafts across sea and river, and overland on sledges hauled by men and oxen.

7,000 years old – suggesting the site has an even longer history. And in 2011, archaeologists discovered a second henge about 900m (3,000ft) away, with a ditch and what appeared to be post-holes. The story is not yet over.

HEALING STONES

The Stonehenge bluestones are mostly dolerite, with four blocks of rhyolite. Each weighs about 4 tonnes. They were brought from the Preseli Hills in Pembrokeshire, where seven stone circles still stand. Some seem to have been chipped, perhaps for slivers that people could take away, and bluestone chips were buried with the dead, suggesting that bluestones were believed to have life-restoring properties.

when Stonehenge took on its most spectacular form. The sarsens, sandstone blocks weighing 25 tonnes, came from the Marlborough Downs 30km (20 miles) away. Four Station Stones marked alignments with moon cycles and midsummer.

Finally, around 1550/1700 BC, the so-called Y and Z holes were set up in two circles outside the sarsens, and the bluestones repositioned, ending up between the Trilithon Horseshoe and the Sarsen Circle. Work then petered out, and the site was finally abandoned.

Many stones fell over or were toppled, possibly by the Romans who decided Stonehenge was a 'Druid stronghold'. Stones were broken up and taken away by local people and visitors. Until 1918, the site was privately owned. It is now a World Heritage Site looked after by English Heritage, and some stones have been straightened and repositioned. In 2008 a mini-excavation, the first since 1964, found charcoal

The Heel Stone marks the original approach to Stonehenge. The name is said to come from an old tale of a monk who was hit on the heel by a stone hurled by the Devil.

Ancient Britain's ritual spaces are full of mystery. That is why so many people visit them, and why some come away with a sense of other-worldliness. We cannot be sure what some of these places looked like, or how they were used. Did a henge form a 'magic circle' for an elite, separated from the everyday world? Or was it a meeting place for all? Did people live in these structures, or gather there at certain times? And why were some of them so big, like the colossal 'super-henges'? Durrington Walls (Wiltshire), built around 2550 BC, was 480m (1,575ft) across, within a chalk bank about 30m (100ft) wide and 3m (10ft) high. Inside were two wooden structures, possibly partly roofed, built about 100 years after the earthwork. The site was big enough to hold 1,500 people.

Near to Durrington Walls is Woodhenge. This smaller wooden structure was discovered in the 1920s from aerial photos that showed buried traces in a wheat field. Woodhenge dates from about 2300 BC, when it was probably a circular wooden building within an earthwork bank and

COMMUNAL LABOUR

Building enormous monuments called for communal effort over many years. At Durrington Walls, for example, it has been estimated that to construct the earthwork would have taken 100 men four years, working a six-day week, and work would have been fitted in alongside farming. Cutting and moving the timber must also have required huge effort, shifting and raising tree trunks weighing 10 tonnes or more.

ditch. Pig bones were found, with cattle bones in the centre, and also the skeleton of a small child with a split skull. This might be evidence of ritual sacrifice, rare in Ancient Britain.

Even more mysterious is the oak stump uncovered by the tide on a Norfolk beach at Holme-next-the-Sea in 1998. Around 4,000 years ago, people had upended the stump of a large oak

➤ A reconstruction of building work at Durrington Walls, showing the builders erecting the timbers for the enclosure.

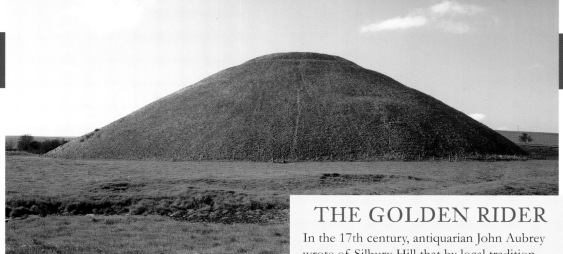

▲ Silbury Hill. After heavy rain in 2000, the top of the mound sank, when an old shaft dug in 1776–77 subsided, leaving a pit 20m (65ft) deep, but this revealed little more about its original use.

➤ An antler-tool found at Silbury Hill in 2001, one of many such tools used by the prehistoric builders to dig out chalk.

THE GOLDEN RIDER

In the 17th century, antiquarian John Aubrey wrote of Silbury Hill that by local tradition 'King Sil, or Zel as the country folk pronounce it, was buried here on horseback'. Legend spoke of a golden rider buried at the heart of the hill. Sadly, exploratory shafts (dug in 1776–77, 1849, 1867 and 1922) found no grave, and neither have more recent excavations. One over-imaginative theory claimed Silbury Hill was the tomb of an Egyptian astronomer-explorer, who did his star-gazing at Stonehenge.

tree (weighing 2 tonnes), and ringed it with 55 oak posts. The media name 'Seahenge' stuck, though this is not a true henge.

The biggest enigma of Ancient Britain, certainly the biggest in volume (35 million basket-loads of chalk), is Silbury Hill in Wiltshire. Europe's largest prehistoric mound, it looms 40m (131ft) above the Bath road in the heart of the Wessex 'ritual landscape', and looks like a burial mound, or even a pyramid. Yet it contains no burials. It may have been a useful lookout post for soldiers in later Roman and early medieval times, but its original purpose hardly seems

military. The mound is a bit like a giant wedding cake, founded on rock with six upper terraces of chalk blocks. At its heart was a cone of clay, which (from the plant and insect remains found in it) was prepared in high summer. So possibly Silbury Hill was a 'harvest hill', linked with a late-summer festival for harvest deities.

◀ Seahenge – not a henge, nor originally in the sea. Dating revealed that the oak stump came from a tree that was felled or died in spring 2050 BC. Some controversy surrounded the removal for conservation of the stump and posts, part of which ended up in King's Lynn Museum in Norfolk.

STANDING STONES

Standing stones can awe even the most worldly visitor, not just by their age, but often also by their location. They can be seen across the British Isles: the Rollright Stones of the Midlands, Stanton Drew in the south-west, Long Meg and her Daughters in Cumbria, the Great Circle at Newgrange in Ireland. Silently eloquent, these stones seem to be signposts on routes we can no longer follow.

There are about a thousand stone circles from north to south across Britain, some in places still remote even in an age when journey times are in hours not weeks. The stone circle at Callanish (Callanais) on the Scottish island of Lewis dates from 2900–2600 BC. Set in a landscape of Neolithic fields and homes were 13 slender stones ringed about a taller central stone 4.75m (13½ft) high. Four avenues (one double, the others single stones) lead off roughly to the four compass points. The southern avenue gives a bearing to the midsummer full moon, setting along distant hilltops in its cycle of 18.6 years.

In Orkney, the Stones of Stenness are among the oldest henge monuments, erected about

▲ Long Meg and her Daughters: a stone circle in Cumbria on the route to the Langdale Pikes axe mines. Long Meg herself stands 3.7m (12ft) tall.

WALKING STONES

Standing stone sites and cairn-circle tombs in Wales include burial chambers such as Pentre Ifan in Pembrokeshire, the Four Stones in Powys and the Druids' Circle in Conwy. In Wales, as elsewhere, legends link stones and water. One legend has it that when the cock crows, the stone at Carreg Bica in West Glamorgan visits the River Neath for a drink, and also bathes in the river on Easter morning.

◄ The Druids' Circle stones (or *Meini Hirion*) in North Wales, built at the crossroads of tracks used in the Bronze Age. Excavations in 1957 uncovered two urns containing the cremated remains of children. One of the stones here is known as the Stone of Sacrifice.

THE BARBER STONE

Around 1325, a local barber-surgeon died at Avebury, probably while helping to bury 'pagan' stones. He was either crushed to death, or collapsed and was buried where he died. In 1938, archaeologists found his bones under a stone, with a purse containing coins dating his unfortunate end, a surgeon's probe and a pair of scissors. The 'Barber Stone' commemorates him.

⋏ The Ring of Brodgar is thought to have been erected between 2500 and 2000 BC. It was built in a true circle, with a diameter measuring 103.6m (340ft).

2500 BC. Four surviving stones, plus stumps and modern markers, delineate its 30-m (98-ft) oval. Inside the oval was a hearth (and probably a two- and a three-stone dolmen). Almost four times bigger but a little younger is the Ring of Brodgar, also in Orkney. There were originally 60 stones in the circle, of which only about half remain.

About 2,600 years ago, people in Wiltshire undertook an enormous project that produced one of the most impressive stone circles: Avebury. The outer Great Circle of about 100 stones is 332m (1,089ft) across, with entrances to the north and south. There are two inner circles; one had 29 stones, the other was a double ring of 27 and 12 stones – though many stones are now missing. The largest still standing is the 65-tonne Swindon Stone in the outer circle. Its partner collapsed in the 18th century, but not before antiquarian William Stukeley (1687–1765) had taken measurements that suggest it weighed around 90 tonnes. In 1723 Stukeley recorded the central obelisk at Avebury to be 21ft (6.4m) high. This stone was later toppled and broken up.

By the 19th century, pillage of stones had reduced Avebury to a dangerous state of desolation. The site was rescued first by Sir John Lubbock (later Lord Avebury) who bought part of the village, and then by marmalade millionaire Alexander Keiller, who purchased Avebury in 1934, excavated and re-erected many stones.

◀ Part of the great circle of standing stones at Avebury, Wiltshire.

BRONZE-AGE BRITAIN

The Bronze Age in Britain, which began roughly about 2300 BC, was a time of cultural exchange across Europe, when metal-using (copper and bronze for tools, gold for wealth) spread quickly. Copper was soft enough to be hammered and could be melted and moulded. Bronze (an alloy of copper and tin) was harder, better for weapons. Yet old Neolithic habits died hard, and flint-working continued until around 500 BC.

Bronze-Age people began burying their dead, important ones anyway, in single graves, with pottery – these are known as 'Beaker burials'. Two styles of pottery were common: two-handled storage jars, and smaller beakers for serving and drinking. The traditional view is that 'Beaker pottery' reached Britain around 2700 BC, and that the 'Beaker people' were migrants or invaders, who brought advanced technology and built stone circles. It seems more likely that Beaker culture spread through trade contacts as well as migration.

Sea voyages were feasible, in boats like the vessel unearthed at Dover (Kent) in 1992. The Dover boat, around 3,550 years old, was made from oak planks, lashed together with twisted yew ropes pushed through holes plugged with wax resin, the plank-seams being sealed with moss and wood strips. Such a boat could have carried a crew of 20 or so across the Channel – on a calm day. Boats have also been found at North Ferriby on Humberside and at Shinewater in Eastbourne, East Sussex.

Swords became the weapon of choice in what was a warrior age. In 1982, a digger gouged up waterlogged timbers from a ditch in Northamptonshire; of late Bronze-Age date, the wood came from an ancient causeway across Flag Fen, near Peterborough. Into the bog people had thrown pottery, bronze daggers and swords – so many swords that most men (presumably) must have owned at least one. Flag Fen also yielded Britain's oldest wooden wheel; made about 1300 BC, it was formed from three sections of alder held together with oak braces and ash pegs. Similar Bronze-Age causeways have been found at Shinewater, and at Fiskerton near Lincoln. Throwing metals into water as an offering continued well into the Iron Age.

▲ A bronze dagger, 33cm (13 inches) long, discovered in its owner's grave. Daggers were less likely to snap than the longer bronze swords that were coming into use at this time.

▼ Bronze-Age pottery featured many examples of beakers, like this one from a burial at Winterslow (Wiltshire).

BRONZE-AGE MINERS

The Great Orme copper mine, on the headland near Llandudno in North Wales, is the biggest Bronze-Age mine in Europe. It was worked from around 1500 BC by miners digging with bone and antler tools, and smashing the limestone rock with stone hammers. Some tunnels are so cramped that only small men, or perhaps children, could have crawled through them.

GRAVE STATUS

Buried close to Stonehenge was the 'Amesbury Archer', so-named because his burial around 2300 BC included arrowheads and wrist-guards. The Archer is thought to have been central European, possibly from Switzerland, and had severe damage to his knee and jaw. The 'healing bluestones' may have drawn him to Stonehenge. Nearby was the grave of a relative, buried with a boar tusk and gold earrings. Was this the princely son of a Bronze-Age king?

Bronze-Age barrow burials often included 'warrior kit' such as a bow, flint-tipped arrows, or a bronze dagger, and some graves show evidence of human sacrifice. During the early Bronze Age, many Neolithic monuments were reworked and enlarged – Stonehenge, for example. This has led to some of the wilder speculations about architects coming to Britain from the Mediterranean, a Wessex aristocracy obsessed with gold, and wizard-priests tapping 'lost knowledge' and 'earth-energy'. The Bronze Age is fertile ground for anyone interested in ley lines, subterranean streams, UFOs, crop circles, astrology and cosmic energy paths, as well as for archaeologists trying to sift fact from fantasy.

▲ Boars' tusks found in the Amesbury Archer's grave were probably symbols of power. The gold hair ornaments from the same burial are among the oldest gold objects found in Britain.

▲ Bronze-Age shears with their wooden holder, from Flag Fen. Other tools found at this site include a flesh-hook for lifting chunks of meat out of a big cooking pot.

◄ The Dover boat can be seen at Dover Museum. This Bronze-Age vessel was made of oak planks without a single nail.

FORTS AND IRON

Iron succeeded bronze as the key tool-making material. Known in the Middle East from 3000 BC, ironworking required much higher levels of expertise and the iron-smith was imbued with magical status. Iron reached central Europe about 900 BC, and Britain by about 700 BC. The Iron Age brought better tools, ploughs – and more deadly weapons. In Iron-Age Britain, people built fortified hilltop settlements to defend their herds and homes.

Around 500 BC, food production was rising. Farmers cleared forests and ploughed heavier soils, using their new iron tools. They grew wheat, barley, oats and rye, along with peas, beans, lentils and flax, and maintained larger herds of cattle, alongside pigs and sheep. They domesticated horses, kept dogs as pets and for hunting, and may also have raised chickens, though this is not certain.

More food meant more people, and the population of Britain may have climbed to 4–5 million by the time the Romans arrived in the 1st century BC, a five-fold increase from the

Neolithic period. There were more villages: at least 3,000 Iron-Age settlements are known, some almost small towns. More trade and foreign contact brought the first use of coins in Britain, after 150 BC, bearing the heads of ruling chiefs, now kings, in the style of the Romanized world.

Hill forts dominated the landscape of southern Britain. Many forts were built on older Neolithic

▲ A reconstruction of an Iron-Age house at Butser Ancient Farm, Hampshire. The thatched roof kept out the weather, but with no windows or chimney the interior must have been dark and smoky.

FORTIFIED NORTHLANDS

North Britain had two typical fortified settlements: the dun in the west and the broch in the north. Duns were clusters of homes enclosed by a stone wall or earth rampart. A broch was a two-storey round tower with no windows, and stairs within the walls leading to the upper floor. There are at least 700 brochs in Scotland, dating from 600 BC to AD 100. In Lowland Scotland people built lake houses called crannogs, round houses on stilts reached by a causeway or by boat.

▲ Iron-craft reached great heights in Iron-Age Britain. The Cookham dagger, with its elegant sheath, was found in the River Thames.

▲ Maiden Castle in Dorset. When occupied, there was a village settlement inside its defences, which were designed to make direct attack difficult, and also symbolized the prestige of the community living here.

➤ The Broch of Mousa, an island off Shetland. Built around 100 BC, the tower-dwelling provided refuge for people, their stores and animals.

campsites. They were formidable rings of ditches and earth banks topped by wooden stakes, with twisting entrances. Maiden Castle in Dorset, the largest hill fort in Britain, has earth ramparts that are still over 6m (20ft) high in parts. Hill forts were places of safety in an age of tribal wars, but also settlements where people lived and traded.

The Romans, who later stormed these hill forts, first learned of Britain through travellers' tales and trade. Recorded around 600 BC as Ierne (Ireland) and Albion (Britain), the islands were called 'Pretanic' by a voyager of 325 BC, and eventually 'Britannia'. Julius Caesar led Roman military expeditions to Britain in 55 and 54 BC, and in AD 43 the Roman army invaded, to make south Britain part of the Roman Empire. North Britain, beyond Hadrian's Wall, remained outside the empire.

With Roman rule came Britain's first written history, but as the centuries passed much of Ancient Britain was lost. In the 16th century, King Henry VIII of England appointed John Leland (1506?–52) to 'search after England's antiquities'. Leland, Britain's first antiquary, was followed by Sir Thomas Browne (1605–82) and John Aubrey (1625–97). Later amateur archaeologists unearthed bones and flint tools, sketched barrows, and dug (usually in vain) for buried treasure. While debating who built Stonehenge or Avebury, people filled in the blanks with colourful speculation, though as the notion of 'prehistory' became current among academics in the 19th century, archaeology became a serious science. Today, modern methods for dating long-buried objects, and techniques for uncovering the past, layer by layer, are helping us to appreciate the achievements of our ancestors, and look afresh at the remarkable heritage of our islands' prehistoric past.

PLACES TO VISIT

Some sites are accessible only on foot, and others (such as Silbury Hill) can only be viewed from a distance, having no direct pedestrian access. Many local museums as well as the great national museum collections have exhibits from Britain's ancient past. All archaeological sites should be regarded as fragile and visited with care and respect. Here is a selection of places to visit.

Ashmolean Museum, Beaumont Street, Oxford OX1 2PH
01865 278002; www.ashmolean.museum.org

British Museum, Great Russell Street, London WC1B 3DG
020 7323 8299; www.britishmuseum.org

Butser Ancient Farm, Chalton, Waterlooville, Hampshire PO8 0BG
023 9259 8838; www.butser.org.uk

Castell Henllys Iron Age Hill Fort, Pembrokeshire Coast National Park
0845 345 7275; www.pembrokeshirecoast.org.uk/default.asp?PID=261

Creswell Crags Museum and Visitor Centre, Derbyshire and Nottinghamshire borders
01909 720378; www.creswell-crags.org.uk

Cheddar Gorge and Caves, Cheddar, Somerset BS27 3QF
01934 742343; www.cheddargorge.co.uk

Dover Museum, Market Square, Dover, Kent CT16 1PB
01304 201066; www.doverdc.co.uk/museum/about_the_museum/visitor_information.aspx

Flag Fen Bronze Age Centre, The Droveway, Peterborough, Cambridgeshire PE6 7QJ
0844 414 0646; www.vivacity-peterborough.com/museums-and-heritage/flag-fen/

Great Orme Mines, Llandudno, North Wales LL30 2XG
01492 870447; http://www.greatormemines.info/

Museum of London, 50 London Wall, London EC2Y 5HN
020 7001 9844; www.museumoflondon.org.uk

National Museum Cardiff, Cathays Park, Cardiff CF10 3NP
029 2039 7951; www.museumwales.ac.uk/en/cardiff/

National Museum of Scotland, Chambers Street, Edinburgh EH1 1JF
0300 123 6789; www.nms.ac.uk/our_museums/national_museum.aspx

Salisbury and South Wiltshire Museum, The Close, Salisbury, Wiltshire SP1 2EN
01722 332151; www.salisburymuseum.org.uk

Star Carr, near Scarborough, North Yorkshire
www.starcarr.com

Wiltshire Heritage Museum, Long Street, Devizes, Wiltshire SN10 1NS
01380 727369; www.wiltshireheritage.org.uk/

National Trust

Avebury, Wiltshire
01762 539250; www.nationaltrust.org.uk/main/w-avebury

ENGLISH HERITAGE

Alexander Keiller Museum, Avebury, Wiltshire SN8 1RF
01672 539250; www.english-heritage.org.uk/daysout/properties/avebury-alexander-keiller-museum/

Castlerigg Stone Circle, Nr Keswick, Cumbria
0870 333 1181; www.english-heritage.org.uk/daysout/properties/castlerigg-stone-circle

Grimes Graves, Lynford, Thetford, Norfolk IP26 5DE
0870 333 1181; www.english-heritage.org.uk/daysout/properties/grimes-graves-prehistoric-flint-mine/

Maiden Castle, Dorset
0870 333 1181; www.english-heritage.org.uk/daysout/properties/maiden-castle/

Stonehenge, Amesbury, Wiltshire SP4 7DE
0870 333 1181; www.english-heritage.org.uk/daysout/properties/stonehenge

West Kennet Long Barrow, Avebury, Wiltshire
0870 333 1181; www.english-heritage.org.uk/daysout/properties/west-kennet-long-barrow/visitor-information

Maeshowe Chambered Cairn, Orkney KW16 3HA
01856 761606; www. historic-scotland.gov.uk and follow Places to Visit link

Ring of Brodgar and Stones of Stenness, near Stromness, Orkney
01856 841815; www.historic-scotland.gov.uk and follow Places to Visit link

Skara Brae Prehistoric Village, Orkney KW16 3LR
01856 841815; www.historic-scotland.gov.uk and follow Places to Visit link

Information correct at time of going to press.

◀ The 'London before London' gallery in the Museum of London explores the prehistory of the area, long before the city began to grow.